THE
LEKACHMACHER
FAMILY

**MADRONA PUBLISHERS, INC.**

Seattle

# THE LEKACHMACHER FAMILY

**Carol Richman**

Library of Congress Cataloging in Publication Data

Richman, Carol, 1924-
    The Lekachmacher family.

    SUMMARY: A Jewish family leaves Russia and persecu-
tion behind to make a new home for themselves in turn-of-
the-century America.

    1. Jews in the United States — Juvenile literature.
2. Lekachmacher family — Juvenile literature.    3. Amer-
icanization — Juvenile literature.    4. United States —
Emigration and immigration — Juvenile literature.    [1.
Jews in the United States.    2. Americanization]    I. Title.
E184.J5R52        973' .04'924        76-23409
ISBN 0-914842-14-5

Once
upon
a
time...

nce upon a time
in a little village
near the city of Minsk,
in the country of Russia,

lived the family Lekachmacher. They were
Jewish people and lived among Jewish people in
a country of Russian people. The Lekachmacher
family made cheese which they sold to the
people who lived in the city of Minsk.

he Lekachmacher family was the father Louis and the mother Kresha and nine children: Samuel, Herman, Isaac, Mosheh, Hannah, Nathan, Jacob, Ruth, and Bessie.

Kresha and Louis cared for their
children. They gave them love
and kept them warm. They
taught them to help and
how to work together.
They took them to schule
and helped them to learn, and
taught them to laugh and sing
and dance. They took them on
walks and to visit their cousins.

**But there was a PROBLEM!**

T here was in the city of Moscow a Czar who was the ruler of all the Russian people. He was a terrible grouch, and he did not like the Jewish people.

(Why do you suppose he did not like the Jewish people? Maybe he did not know them. Maybe he did not like them because they were different. They prayed differently and they looked different.)

**W**orking for the Czar were a lot of soldiers called the Cossacks, and they did not like the Jews, either. They would ride their horses into where the Jews lived and trample the chickens and the gardens, they would bother the girls, and they would try to catch the young men to make them soldiers, too.

(It was very unpleasant and scary for the Lekachmacher family and the other Jewish people to have the Czar, the soldiers, and many other Russian people not like them.)

**A**nd things were getting worse! Every day, visitors to the village where the Lekachmachers lived brought news about bad things that were happening to Jews. Louis and Kresha were very upset. They were afraid that the soldiers would come and

take their grown-up sons
Samuel, Herman, and Isaac and
put them in the army and not be
nice to them. They called their
sons to them to talk about what
to do. They could not hide. They
would have to go away to
another place.

ut where could they go? "To America," cried Isaac. "It is too far," said Kresha. Louis said, "We do not have enough money." "We would be safe in America," Herman said. "I know what we should do," said Samuel. "We three will go first, and we will work hard in America and send back money

for you all to come." Kresha cried, but they all agreed that that was what they had to do. Kresha and Louis thought of all the dangers. The sons thought of the many nice things they might find in America.

Everybody was very sad that Samuel, Herman, and Isaac were leaving. But the whole family helped them get ready—washing and mending the best clothes and packing them in the carpetbag suitcases which Louis had bought for the trip. The brothers said goodby to their friends. Louis and Kresha gave the money for the trip to the oldest son, Samuel, to carry.

aying goodby was very hard. Kresha and Louis and Hannah cried. Mosheh and Nathan were too big to cry and just frowned. Jacob, Ruth, and Bessie cried. Samuel, Herman, and Isaac were very brave and told their mother and father and the children not to worry because they would all be coming to America soon, and they would be together again. The three sons hugged and kissed everyone goodby and set off on their long journey to the seaport where they got on a boat to sail and sail across the ocean.

Many people were going to America from many different countries and on many ships.

Some, like Samuel, Herman, and Isaac, were Jews looking for a place where they could live in freedom. Others who had been hungry and poor in their old countries were looking for a country where they would no longer be poor. All of the people who were coming to America were looking for a new and better life in their new country. They were excited, but they were also afraid because they did not know what it would be like in America.

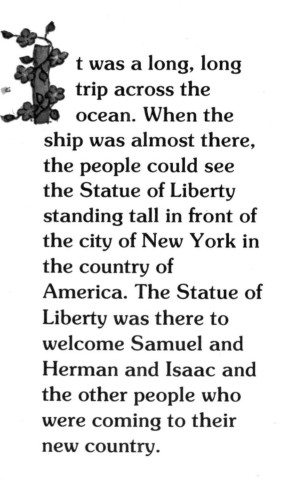

t was a long, long trip across the ocean. When the ship was almost there, the people could see the Statue of Liberty standing tall in front of the city of New York in the country of America. The Statue of Liberty was there to welcome Samuel and Herman and Isaac and the other people who were coming to their new country.

The writing on
the Statue
said:

Give me your tired, your poor,
your huddled masses yearning
    to breathe free,
the wretched refuse of
    your teeming shore,
send these, the homeless,
    tempest-tossed, to me:
I lift my lamp beside the
    golden door.

The people smiled with tears in their eyes. Samuel, Herman, and Isaac thought of the day when their mother and father and sisters and brothers would also come to their new country.

amuel, Herman, and Isaac had a lot of things to do when they got to America. They had a lot of things to see in their strange new country. They walked in the streets of New York City and looked at the people and the buildings and heard the strange new language.

They had to find a place to live and jobs to work at. They had to learn the language.

They had to learn the ways to live in America—the foods to eat and the clothes to wear, how to find their way around to the stores and the parks and the library. They had to make new friends and understand the laws, hear the music, see the games.

And while they were learning new things, they were working hard at their jobs and saving their money to send back to Louis and Kresha. They missed their mother and father and brothers and sisters very much.

**M**eanwhile, back in Russia the family waited and saved. One day after a long time, Louis counted the money and said they had enough! Everyone was very glad because they missed Samuel, Herman, and Isaac very much, but also because things were still bad for Jews in Russia.

It was an exciting and busy time getting ready. But Kresha and Louis were very sad to be leaving their old home and friends and relatives and everything they had always known. They could not carry very much with them besides their clothes. They had to leave their furniture and toys.

They started on the long trip, first to the boat and then across the ocean. They sailed and sailed and finally they came to America. Samuel, Herman, and Isaac met them at the boat, and they were all so happy! They all went to the place that would be their new home. When they sat down to dinner they gave their thanks that the whole family was together and safe in America.

**I**n America everyone could laugh without being afraid. The family was happy to be together and safe in the new country. They wanted to learn the ways of America. They made their names more American.

Lekachmacher became Lekachman. Isaac was called Bill. Mosheh became Morris. Hannah became Ann. Jacob was Jack. Ruth was Billie, and Bessie became Betty.

They were learning the new
language, new ways to dress
and eat. They were happy.

THEN—
**something very sad
happened.**

Louis got very sick and died. Kresha loved him so much that very soon she died, too, of a broken heart. What were the children to do with both of their parents gone?

**A**ll the children cried and cried, but Samuel said and Herman said and Ann said: "We must be brave and strong and take care of each other." Samuel, Herman, Bill, and Morris said: "We will work and buy food and clothes." Ann said: "I will take care of the house and the children." Nat, Billie, and Betty said: "We will be very good and help," and they all did.

The nine children loved each other and took care of each other. They liked their new country more and more and were becoming more American and forgetting Russia. The children went to school. Everyone worked hard, and everyone studied to learn to speak English and to learn about America. They learned the games and the songs and the dances and made new friends. They thanked God that they were safe in America.

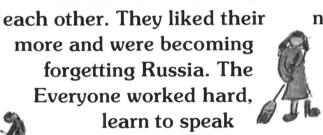

s time went on, the children grew older, and pretty soon the brothers and sisters began to get married. Samuel and Herman, Bill and Morris.

When Ann got married and went to live far away in Wisconsin she took Betty, who was still too young to live by herself. Nat and

Jack and Billie got married, and now everyone was married except Betty.

(Like many other people who came to America from other countries, the brothers and sisters moved to different places in America.)

fter a while, Betty fell in love and got married. She and her husband went to live in a home of their own and had two children. After a long time, those children grew up and got married and had children of their own.

NOW those children are grown up. Do you know the rest?

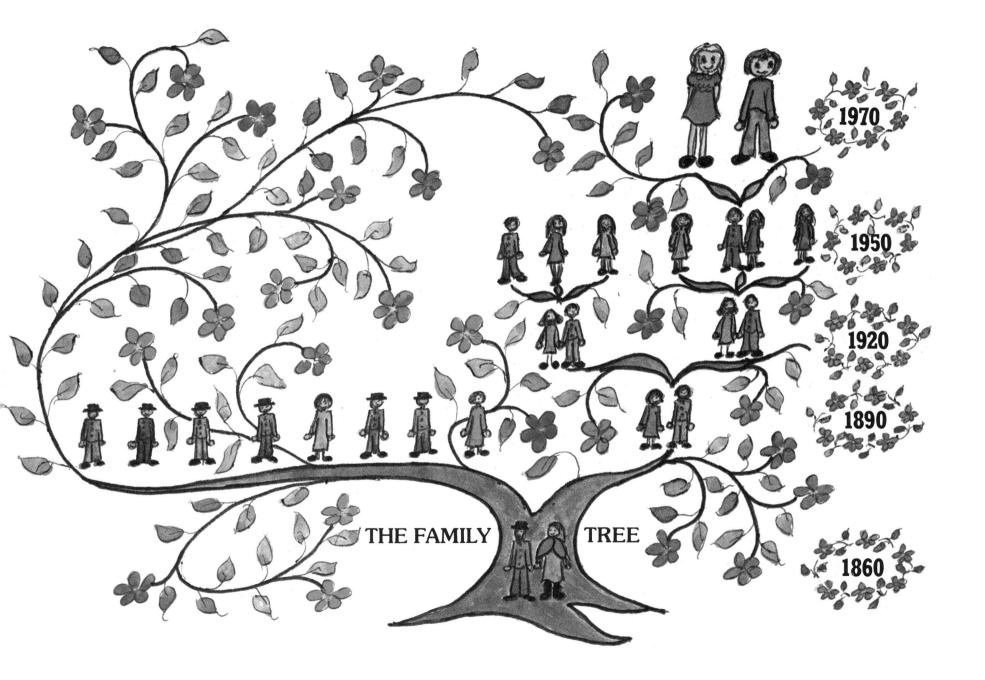

THE FAMILY TREE

1970

1950

1920

1890

1860